· MEET ·
CLAUDE MONET

Read with You Center for Excellence in STEAM Education

Read With You

ISBN: 979-8-88618-081-7
First Edition January 2022

Woman with a Parasol, Madame Monet and Her Son, 1875

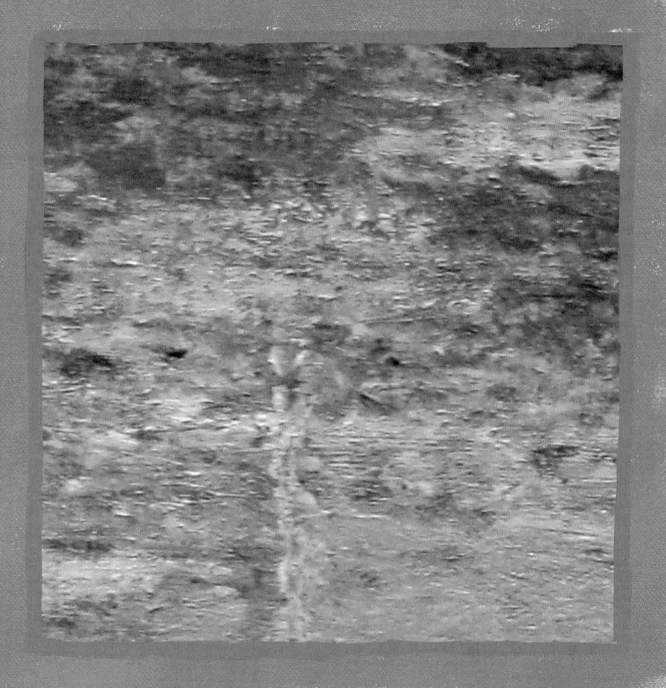

I love boats on the water.
Do you think you can sail through a painting?

Red Boats at Argenteuil, 1875

The Houses of Parliament, 1903-1904

Poppy Fields near Argenteuil, 1875

Cliffs at Pourville, 1882

Nympheas, 1897-1898

Water Lilies and Japanese Bridge, 1899

Garden at Sainte-Adresse, 1867

Find Examples

This is part of a painting titled *Vétheuil in Summer* (1880).

Choose one of the big clouds and count how many brushstrokes are in it.

Look at the tall trees. How are the tree brushstrokes different from the sky brushstrokes?

Can you find the little people in the painting?

What are they doing?

Connect

This painting is titled *The Geese* (1874).

Where does the water start and end in this painting?

What sounds would you hear if you were sitting near the water?

What time of the year is it? How do you know?

Using your finger, copy the brushstrokes Monet used on the leaves. Can you make short little flicks?

Craft

Option 1

1. Look at the clouds in Monet's paintings.

2. Choose your favorite blue and white paints and find paper to paint on.

3. Paint the top half of your piece of paper blue for the sky. Then, try painting clouds like Monet, with big, fat brushstrokes!

4. What else would you like to add to your picture?

Option 2

1. Think of your favorite outdoor place to go, like a beach or a park.

2. Draw a big picture of this place.

3. Add some tiny people to your picture to show the size of your place!

Made in the USA
Monee, IL
08 January 2025